Our World

SEAS AND OCEANS

David Lambert

Silver Burdett Press
Morristown, New Jersey

Titles in this series

Deserts

Jungles and Rainforests

Mountains

Polar Regions

Rivers and Lakes

Seas and Oceans

First published in 1987 by
Wayland (Publishers) Ltd
61 Western Road, Hove
East Sussex BN3 1JD

Adapted and first published
in the United States in 1988
by Silver Burdett Press
Morristown, New Jersey

Edited by Francesca Motisi

U.S. edition edited by Joanne Fink

Designed by Malcolm Smythe and Alison Leggate

Library of Congress Cataloging-in-Publication Data

Lambert, David, 1932–
    Seas and oceans / David Lambert.
        p. cm. — (Our world)
    Bibliography: p.
    Includes index.
    Summary: Examines the world's oceans, their physical features, movements, plant and animal life, and relationship with humanity.
        ISBN 0–382–09503–0 (lib. bdg.) : $12.96
        1. Ocean—Juvenile literature. [1. Ocean.] I. Title. II. Series.
GC21.5.L34 1988
551.46—dc19

Typeset by DP Press, Sevenoaks, Kent
Printed in Italy by G. Canale & C.S.p.A., Turin.

Front cover, main picture Atlantic Ocean waves crash into the beach on the coast of New Jersey.
Front cover, inset Diver photographing crinoid on orange sponge, Bonaire, Lesser Antilles.
Back cover Gathering seaweed, Japan.

Contents

Chapter 1   Our watery world

The world's seas and oceans   4
Sea water and sea ice   6

Chapter 2   The restless sea

Waves   8
Tides   10
Currents   12
Oceans grow and shrink   14

Chapter 3   Sea and land

Coasts   16
Ocean floor   18
Islands   20

Chapter 4   Life in the sea

Life near the surface   22
Deep-sea life   24
Life inshore   26

Chapter 5   Understanding the sea

Exploring underwater   28

Chapter 6   People and the sea

The Polynesians of the Pacific   30
Ships and shipping   32
Food from the sea   34
Mining the sea   36

Chapter 7   Tomorrow's seas and oceans

Seas in danger   38
Saving the sea   40
Harnessing seas and oceans   42

Glossary   45

Further reading   46

Index   47

The world's seas and oceans

If a spaceman looked down upon our earth he would see mainly water. Our planet is unlike any other as it holds nearly all the liquid water in the solar system. Most of the water is contained within the oceans, the remaining few percent being in lakes, rivers, and ice caps. It is because of this that the earth is sometimes called "the water planet."

In the rest of the universe matter tends to be hot gases or frozen solids; so our oceans only exist because the earth's surface temperature is in the very narrow range in which water remains liquid. Salty water covers about seven parts in ten of the earth's surface. In fact its southern half is four parts water for every one part land.

This water fills four huge hollows in the earth's surface, and it is these water-filled hollows that form the Pacific, Atlantic, Indian, and Arctic oceans. Between the oceans are vast land masses called continents. No continent completely separates one ocean from another, but bays and islands mark off parts of oceans into smaller areas called seas. However, the Caspian Sea in the Soviet Union, and the Dead Sea, on the border of Israel and Jordan, are salty inland lakes.

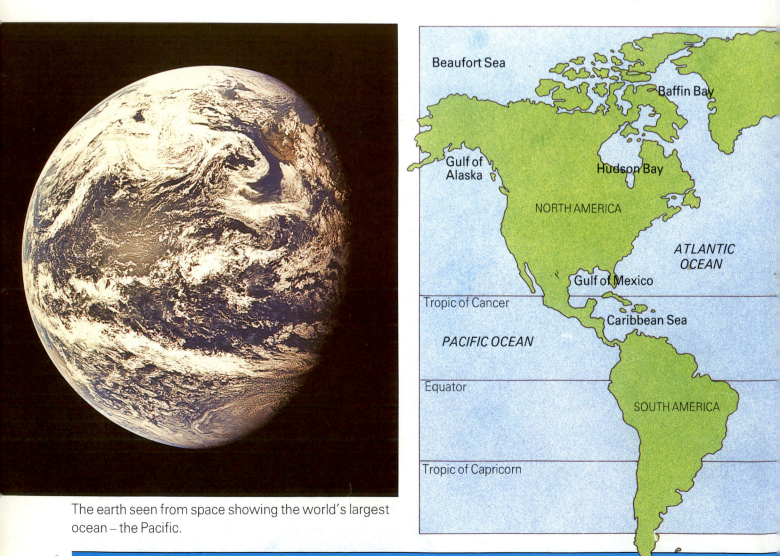

The earth seen from space showing the world's largest ocean – the Pacific.

The Pacific Ocean is the largest ocean. This body of water could hold all the continents and almost all three other oceans. It spreads nearly half way around the world, from Asia east to the Americas, and from Antarctica north almost to the Arctic. The Pacific is also the deepest ocean. The world's highest peak, Mount Everest, would disappear if dropped into the Pacific's Philippine Trench, which is 32,995 feet deep.

The Atlantic Ocean lies east of the Americas and west of Europe and Africa. This is the second largest ocean, only half the size of the Pacific. Yet it has the longest coasts and includes two of the world's largest seas: the Caribbean and the Mediterranean.

The Indian Ocean ranks third for size. But if you could iron out its floor it would be deeper than the Atlantic. The continents that form its rim are Africa, Asia, Australia, and Antarctica.

The smallest, shallowest ocean is the cold Arctic Ocean in the far north of the world. More than thirteen oceans of its size would fit into the Pacific, and the Arctic Ocean's average depth is only one quarter that of the Pacific.

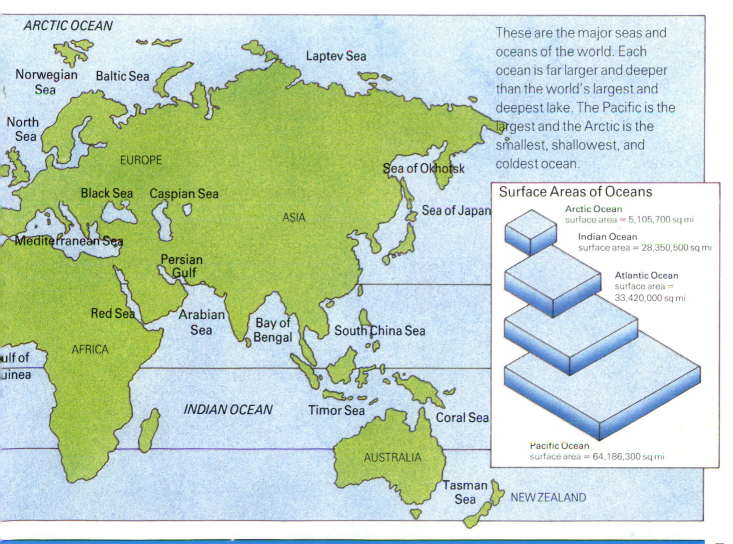

ARCTIC OCEAN

Laptev Sea

Norwegian Sea

Baltic Sea

North Sea

EUROPE

Sea of Okhotsk

Black Sea

Caspian Sea

ASIA

Sea of Japan

Mediterranean Sea

Persian Gulf

Red Sea

Arabian Sea

Bay of Bengal

South China Sea

Gulf of Guinea

AFRICA

INDIAN OCEAN

Timor Sea

Coral Sea

AUSTRALIA

Tasman Sea

NEW ZEALAND

These are the major seas and oceans of the world. Each ocean is far larger and deeper than the world's largest and deepest lake. The Pacific is the largest and the Arctic is the smallest, shallowest, and coldest ocean.

Surface Areas of Oceans

Arctic Ocean surface area = 5,105,700 sq mi

Indian Ocean surface area = 28,350,500 sq mi

Atlantic Ocean surface area = 33,420,000 sq mi

Pacific Ocean surface area = 64,186,300 sq mi

Sea water and sea ice

Millions of years ago there were no seas or oceans. The surface of the earth was so hot that water boiled away. But volcanoes poured huge amounts of steam into the atmosphere. Then the earth cooled down. Steam turned to water vapor that condensed as droplets which began to fall as rain. This downpour lasted for many thousands of years, filling great hollows in the land and thus forming the world's first seas.

Even now, vast quantities of water evaporate from seas and oceans. In air the water vapor cools, then clouds form and shed their moisture as rain, snow, sleet, and hail. Most falls right back into the sea. The rest is carried there by rivers flowing off the land. So sea water keeps going round and round. This process is called the water cycle.

But oceans hold more than water. They contain salts and minerals dissolved from rocks below the sea and washed into the sea by rivers. Three-quarters of all sea salt is the kind we use to flavor food. The salt in the sea is made up of many substances but common salt (sodium chloride) is the most abundant.

Some seas are saltier than others. Where rivers flow into the sea the amount of salt is lower than in the open seas. For example, at the mouth of the Amazon the sea is fresh for almost 100 miles from the delta. The amount of salt in the Red Sea is very high, as it is an almost enclosed area where little water flows from the land, and the sun evaporates the water very quickly. However, the water in the Dead Sea is five times as salty as in the Red Sea, and so salty that only a few kinds of animals and plants can survive in it.

Saltiness is only one of several differences. Tropical waters like the Red Sea are far warmer

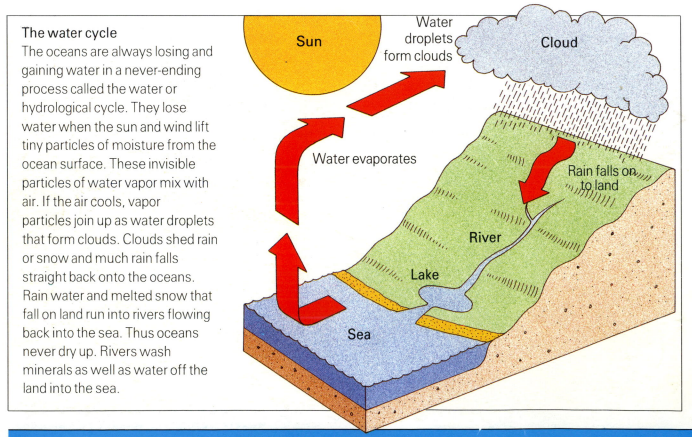

The water cycle
The oceans are always losing and gaining water in a never-ending process called the water or hydrological cycle. They lose water when the sun and wind lift tiny particles of moisture from the ocean surface. These invisible particles of water vapor mix with air. If the air cools, vapor particles join up as water droplets that form clouds. Clouds shed rain or snow and much rain falls straight back onto the oceans. Rain water and melted snow that fall on land run into rivers flowing back into the sea. Thus oceans never dry up. Rivers wash minerals as well as water off the land into the sea.

Sun

Water droplets form clouds

Cloud

Water evaporates

Rain falls on to land

River

Lake

Sea

Icebergs are chunks of land ice that have broken off into the sea. This huge iceberg is in Disco Bay, Greenland.

than polar waters like the Arctic Ocean. More than one in ten parts of the world's total oceanic surface is covered by ice. Some of this is frozen sea water and the rest is land ice which has flowed into the sea. Icebergs are chunks of land ice that have broken off into the sea. In summer, winds, currents, and tides break up much of the sea ice, which is then carried away as ice floes. Icebergs and ice floes drift according to the wind and currents. Some icebergs are so huge that they drift into warmer waters before they melt.

Deep down all seas and oceans are very cold. Also, the deeper a diver descends, the darker it becomes and the harder water presses on his body. Scuba divers breathe bottled air at the same high pressure as the water around them. On the ocean floor, water pressure may be up to a thousand times greater than pressure at the surface.

These people are enjoying themselves in the clear, warm, tropical sea in Barbados.

Waves

Seas and oceans are never still. Water is always on the move, below or at the surface.

Moving air stirs up the surface waters. Even a gentle breeze forms patches of tiny ripples called catspaws. A stronger wind builds waves. Waves are parallel rows of watery ridges with watery valleys in between. The ridges are called wave crests, the valleys are troughs. Crests and troughs follow one another through the sea.

In the open ocean, waves only seem to carry water with them. In fact each wave crest sets water particles circling. As the crest passes, particles are lifted and moved briefly forward, then they sink down and back. That is why a seagull bobs up and down on the sea instead of moving with the waves.

Inshore, however, waves behave differently. When a wave reaches shallow water, some of its circling water particles hit the seabed, so the bottom of the wave slows down. But the wave crest carries on until it topples forward and breaks upon the shore.

The stronger the wind, the larger waves become. Waves are measured by their height and length. Wave height is the height from a wave trough to the next wave crest. Wave length is the distance between two crests. The longest waves form where strong winds blow for a long time across a great stretch of open ocean. Here, rounded waves called swells can reach a wave length of over half a mile. Where storm waves near a coast, they may tower as high as 111 feet.

Some of the highest waves are set off not by wind but by underwater earthquakes or volcanoes. These waves are called *tsunamis*. Tsunamis race across the Pacific Ocean at up to 500 miles an hour. Where they reach shallow bays their wave height can reach 220 feet. Tsunamis sometimes sweep inland and drown whole villages.

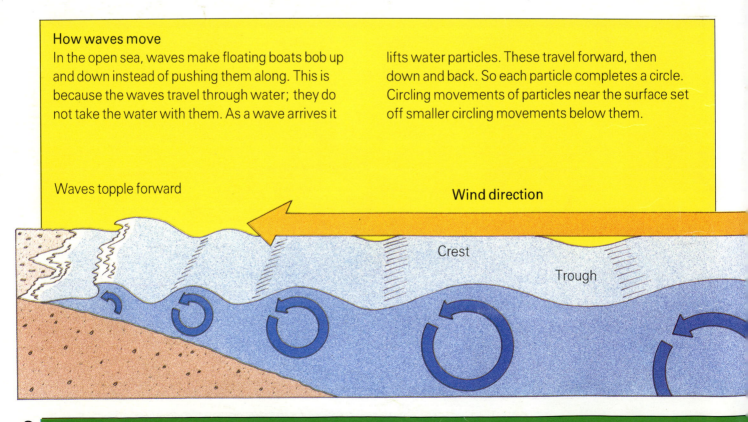

How waves move

In the open sea, waves make floating boats bob up and down instead of pushing them along. This is because the waves travel through water; they do not take the water with them. As a wave arrives it lifts water particles. These travel forward, then down and back. So each particle completes a circle. Circling movements of particles near the surface set off smaller circling movements below them.

Waves topple forward

Wind direction

Crest

Trough

Waves breaking on the shore at Kynance Cove in Cornwall, England.

Tides

Tides are the slow, steady rise and fall of the surface of the sea that goes on every day. Water creeps up a beach to reach its highest level, called high tide. Then it slips back to its lowest level, called low tide.

Tides are really huge, slow waves that travel around the oceans twice a day. In that time the moon orbits the earth once. The moon's huge pulling power, or gravitation, is the main force that keeps tides on the move. The moon pulls oceans toward it on the earth's moon-facing side. Meanwhile, on the far side, the earth's spin tries to throw water outward. These two "waves" travel around the earth, following the moon. Each wave crest is a high tide, each wave trough, a low tide.

Tides do not happen as you might expect. The continents, underwater ridges, the earth's spin, and the sun's pulling force all interfere with them.

Different parts of one ocean can have separate tidal systems. Most shores have two high tides a day, but Alaska and the Gulf of Mexico get only one. The Baltic and Mediterranean seas, almost cut off from the open ocean, have scarcely any tides at all. But the sea can rise twice as high as a house at high tide in Canada's long, narrow Bay of Fundy. Look at the photographs on the right.

On most shores tides vary with the time of month. Extra high, high tides and extra low, low tides happen when the sun and moon line up to pull together on the oceans. Such tides are known as spring-tides. When sun and moon pull at right angles to each other they tend to cancel one another out. This gives neap-tides, with low, high tides and high, low tides. Each type of tide comes roughly twice a month.

The restless tides

Tides are set in motion mostly by the moon. The moon's pulling power, or gravitation, is the main force that keeps tides on the move. As the moon orbits the earth its gravitational pull tugs part of the ocean surface toward it, so the ocean surface bulges out toward the moon. The bulge travels around the world, following the moon. The spinning motion of the earth produces another bulge, on the side of the world opposite the first bulge. The bulges bring high tides. The troughs between them bring low tides. Changing positions of sun and moon cause spring-tides at new (and full) moon; neap-tides at half moon.

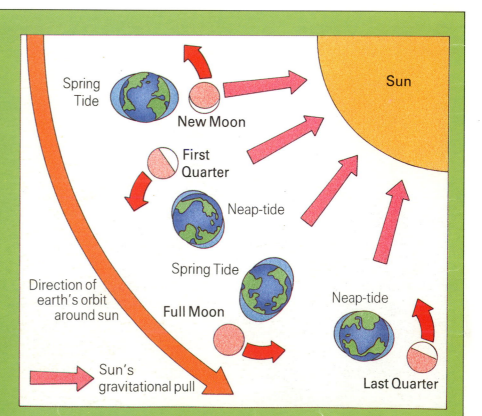

The main picture shows high tide at the Bay of Fundy in Canada. The inset picture shows the same bay at low tide.

Currents

Currents are great bands of water flowing through the oceans like rivers. The famous Gulf Stream current is up to 37 miles wide, 2600 feet deep, and in some places may travel more than 60 miles in a day.

Strong winds keep surface currents on the move. The trade winds of the tropics tend to push water from east to west. Near the cold polar regions, westerly winds push the water from west to east. But currents get turned aside by continents. Then, too, the earth's spin deflects currents from their windblown paths. North of the equator, currents bend to the right. South of the equator they bend to the left. This is called the Coriolis effect after its discoverer, the French mathematician Gaspard de Coriolis.

Winds, continents, and the Coriolis effect make currents flow around the oceans in huge loops named gyres. In the northern hemisphere their water travels clockwise; in the southern hemisphere it travels counter-clockwise. In the North Atlantic gyre, the North Equatorial Current flows west, north of the equator toward the Caribbean Sea and Gulf of Mexico. From here, the warm, fast-flowing Gulf Stream heads northeast past the eastern United States. Then it weakens and

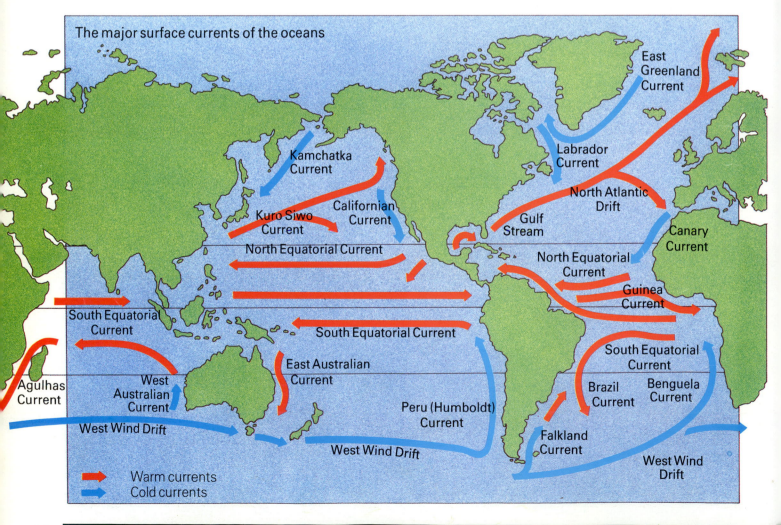

The major surface currents of the oceans

East Greenland Current
Kamchatka Current
Labrador Current
North Atlantic Drift
Kuro Siwo Current
Californian Current
Gulf Stream
North Equatorial Current
Canary Current
North Equatorial Current
Guinea Current
South Equatorial Current
South Equatorial Current
South Equatorial Current
Agulhas Current
West Australian Current
East Australian Current
Peru (Humboldt) Current
Brazil Current
Benguela Current
West Wind Drift
West Wind Drift
Falkland Current
West Wind Drift

➡ Warm currents
➡ Cold currents

divides. One part, called the North Atlantic Drift, carries warm water northeast to the British Isles and Norway; this is the main cause of the mild winter climate of northwest Europe. A southern branch, called the Canaries Current, collects cold water rising from deep down and brings it south to northwest Africa. Then it joins the east end of the North Equatorial Current, and so completes the North Atlantic gyre.

Warm tropical currents take heat from the equator north and south to cooler regions. Meanwhile, cold, heavy water sinks in polar oceans, then flows along the ocean floor back to the tropics.

Currents flow on the surface of the sea and deep down. This diver is monitoring the current flow with dye.

Below South Devon in England is warmed by the North Atlantic Drift, which results in semi-tropical vegetation.

Oceans grow and shrink

The shapes and sizes of the oceans are always slowly changing. This is because of how the surface of the earth is made. The hard rocks of the continents and ocean floor form the earth's crust. And this floats on a thick layer of dense, hot rock called the mantle. Scientists believe currents of hot rock rise like molasses through the mantle until they hit the crust. Then each current divides into two currents. These tug apart the crust above, especially where it is thin, below the oceans. This has opened cracks that divide the earth's crust into huge jigsaw pieces called plates.

Below the oceans molten rock keeps welling up and sticking to both edges of the crack between two plates. Molten rock built the Mid-Atlantic Ridge, an underwater mountain chain astride a crack that splits the Atlantic Ocean down the middle. From such spreading ridges, new ocean floor keeps growing sideways.

But where two crustal plates collide, one plate gets forced below the other, and old ocean floor plunges down into the mantle. This happens in deep ocean trenches. In time it seems all ocean floor gets gobbled up this way.

Over many millions of years these changes gradually alter the sizes, shapes, and positions of land and sea. Long ago there was a single continent called Pangaea, surrounded by one mighty ocean. Today, the Atlantic Ocean is growing wider and the Pacific Ocean is shrinking, although oceans grow or shrink by only an inch or so each year.

Meanwhile, the ocean level has been changing, too. A million years ago ice sheets held so much of the world's water that the ocean level fell. Dry land linked Asia and America. When the ice sheets started melting, the ocean level rose. Sea separated Asia from America, and parts of mainland Europe and Asia became cut off as islands.

Other changes have occurred when shallow seas invaded continents. The Black Sea and Caspian Sea are the remains of a vast sea that once stretched from central Europe to central Asia.

A cross-section through the ocean floor

This diagram shows two oceanic crustal plates separating in mid-ocean. There, molten rock wells up through the gap between the plates to form a spreading ridge. This is where new ocean floor is always being made. But currents in the mantle help to tug both oceanic plates apart. So new ocean floor moves slowly away from the spreading ridge. After many million years the moving ocean floor meets a crustal plate that supports a continent. The oceanic plate is forced down beneath the continental plate into the mantle. There, the oceanic crust will melt.

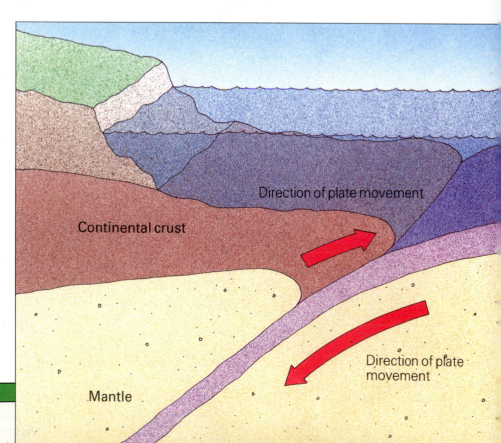

Direction of plate movement

Continental crust

Direction of plate movement

Mantle

Raised beaches caused by land uplift can be found in many parts of the world. These fields on the Devon coast near Salcombe, England, were once a beach.

These coral heads on Isabela Island, in the Galapagos Islands, were upraised in 1954 by an average of fifteen feet. The volcano Fernandina is in the background.

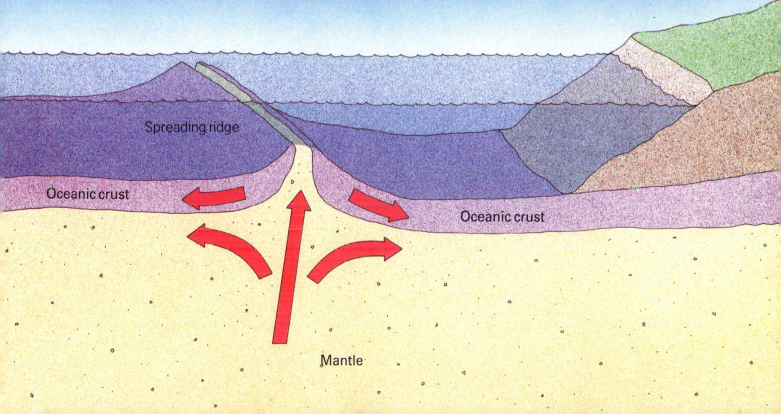

Spreading ridge

Oceanic crust

Oceanic crust

Mantle

Coasts

Where sea meets land the two fight a long, slow war. On some stretches of coast, waves are eating away great chunks of land. But not far away, land might be pushing out into the sea.

If a coast is formed of rocks or cliffs you can be sure the sea is winning. On stormy days waves crash against the shore and punch air into cracks in rocks. As waves retreat this squashed air expands. These sudden changes loosen chunks of rock. Now and then they topple down into the sea.

Next, waves pound these rocks against each other and the sea-bed. This pounding splits the broken rocks into stones. Storm waves then smash them hard against the shore.

The sea's attack gradually cuts a notch in the bottom of a sea cliff, and makes the cliff top-heavy.

Hard rock juts out into the sea as peninsulas, like Hartland Quay in Devon, England.

Formation of a coastline

Waves carrying bits of broken rock crash against a sloping rocky coast. In time the sea wears away enough rock to cut a notch into the shore, between the levels of low tide and high tide.

The notch gets deeper as the sea eats away more land. Nothing now supports the rock above the notch. When this overhanging rock falls into the sea the sloping coast becomes a steep sea cliff.

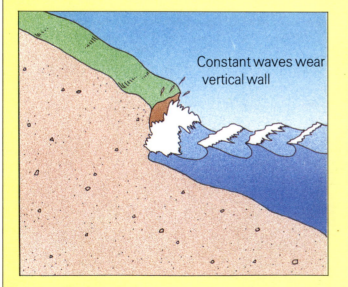

Constant waves wear vertical wall

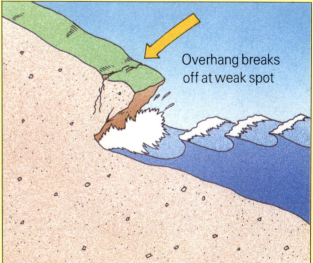

Overhang breaks off at weak spot

In time its front edge falls into the sea. Bit by bit, more cliff is lost. But waves attack soft rocks more easily than hard ones. So deep bays form where soft rock has been gnawed away. Between bays, peninsulas of hard rock still stick out into the sea, as the photograph on the left shows.

Meanwhile new land is formed. First, waves and currents drag scraps of broken rock along the shore. Then they drop this load in calm offshore water. In the same way, rivers shed huge loads of mud in sheltered estuaries. The scraps of rock build sand or gravel beaches. The mud piles up to form low mudflats peeping above the sea. If plants grow on a beach or mudflat, their roots help to stop it from being washed away by storms. So some beaches and mudflats slowly build land out into the sea.

Rivers drop large amounts of mud in estuaries. The mud accumulates, eventually forming mudflats.

In this scene, waves have cut an arch right through the end of a cliff that forms a peninsula. Storm waves have opened a blowhole in the clifftop. In wild weather sea water bursts up through the hole.

The sea now gnaws away the foot of the cliff and attacks any weakness in the cliff face. Bit by bit, waves loosen the rock on each side of a crack. Bits of rock drop, and the crack widens.

Years later, the arch roof has collapsed. Now sea separates the tip of the cliff from the mainland. The tip has become a tiny, steep, offshore island. Such islands are called stacks.

Waves undercut rocks

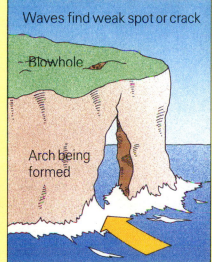

Waves find weak spot or crack

Blowhole

Arch being formed

Stack

Ocean floor

We now know that oceans as well as continents have mountain peaks and valleys. Imagine an underwater trip from Europe across the Atlantic Ocean to the West Indies.

First you cross a broad, shallow platform called a continental shelf. This juts many miles into the sea, yet lies no more than 600 feet below the waves. The shelf's floor has a covering of gravel, sand, and mud washed off the land by rivers, tides, and currents. Continental shelves rim every continent, though some are narrower than others.

Next, the shelf ends and you slide down a long, long continental slope to the bottom of the open ocean, about 12,500 feet deep. Here and there the slope is split by earthquakes and gashed by sliding sediments dropped by river water flowing far out to the sea. Such sediments pile up below the continental slope to form a gentler slope known as the continental rise. Now come vast deep-sea plains and mountains. More than half the earth's surface consists of this immense abyss. Its blanket of soft ooze is largely made of billions of tiny skeletons of plants and creatures that have died and settled on the ocean floor.

In mid ocean, a long climb takes you across the great volcanic Mid-Atlantic Ridge – part of the longest mountain chain on earth. Its highest peaks stick up above the sea as Iceland, the Azores, and other islands.

Beyond these mountains you reach another deep-sea plain. Then, suddenly, the sea bed tilts sharply down into the Puerto Rico Trench. This narrow slit contains the deepest sea floor anywhere in the Atlantic Ocean. But just beyond, the sea bed rises sharply to the big West Indies islands and your journey's end.

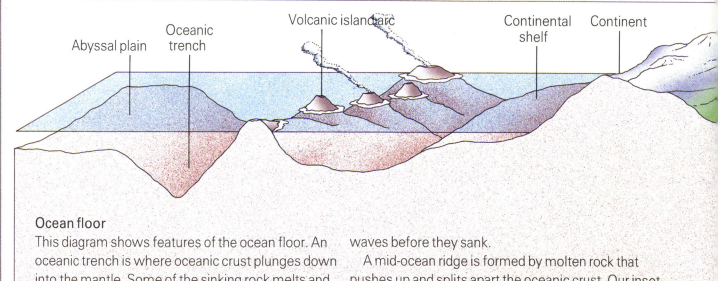

Abyssal plain Oceanic trench Volcanic island arc Continental shelf Continent

Ocean floor

This diagram shows features of the ocean floor. An oceanic trench is where oceanic crust plunges down into the mantle. Some of the sinking rock melts and bobs up through the continental crust to form a curved row of volcanic islands called an island arc. Most oceanic islands are volcanoes. Guyots are drowned volcanoes whose tops were cut off by the waves before they sank.

A mid-ocean ridge is formed by molten rock that pushes up and splits apart the oceanic crust. Our inset diagram shows details of the ridge. Raised, tilted blocks of crust flank a central rift valley. Cracks called transverse faults cut across the valley and the raised blocks.

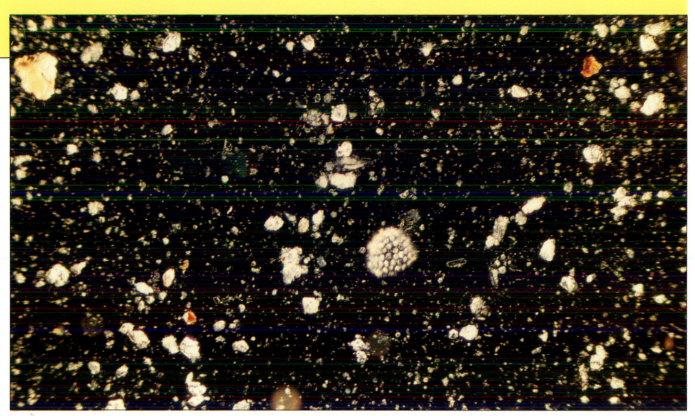

Much ooze is made of billions of tiny skeletons of plants and creatures that died and settled on the ocean floor.

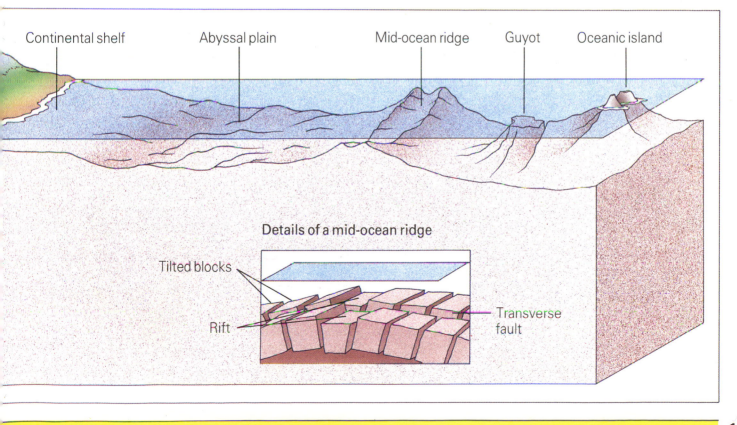

Continental shelf   Abyssal plain   Mid-ocean ridge   Guyot   Oceanic island

Details of a mid-ocean ridge

Tilted blocks

Rift

Transverse fault

Islands

Islands large and small lie scattered through the oceans. The biggest are two southern island continents, Antarctica and Australia. Many millions of years ago these broke away from what was then the world's one continent, Pangaea. A process called continental drift slowly shifted them to where they stand today. In much the same way, the huge northern island, Greenland, split away from North America. Greenland is the largest island that is not a continent. Movements of the earth's crust also probably tore New Zealand's islands from Australia, and ripped Japan from mainland Asia.

Many more big islands once belonged to nearby continents. Borneo, Java, and Sumatra were parts of Sundaland, a huge peninsula of Southeast Asia. Ireland and Great Britain were once attached to the rest of Europe. About 10,000 years ago, the rising level of the sea began to cut off all these lands from one another and their continental mainlands.

Thousands of volcanic islands stand far out in the Atlantic, Indian, and Pacific oceans. They formed from molten rock that poured from holes or cracks in the ocean floor, then piled up, cooled, and hardened. The Hawaiian Islands popped up, one by one, in a straight line. Many Caribbean and North Pacific islands form curved rows that sprouted near an oceanic trench. Some oceanic islands are brand new. For instance, Lateika first poked its fiery head above the Pacific Ocean in the 1970s.

In time, many volcanic islands sink below the sea. Meanwhile, small sea creatures may build an atoll on its disappearing rim. An atoll is a reef of low, limy rock surrounding a lagoon. The coral often grows upward as fast as the volcano sinks.

Coral reefs grow only in shallow, warm, clear water. Some fringe mainland shores. The Great Barrier Reef sprawls for more than 1200 miles along Australia's Queensland coast. It is a collection of coral reefs and islands that forms an immense natural breakwater.

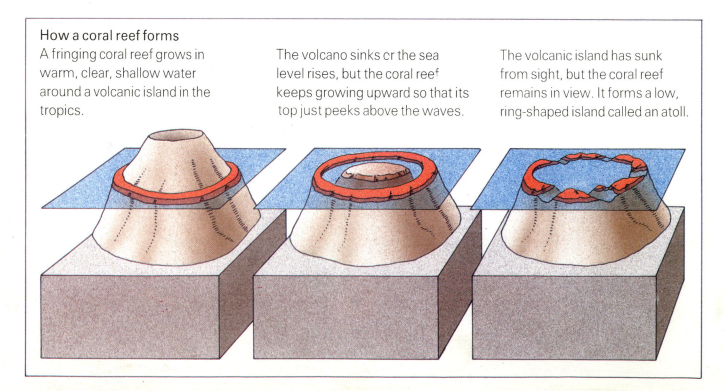

How a coral reef forms

A fringing coral reef grows in warm, clear, shallow water around a volcanic island in the tropics.

The volcano sinks cr the sea level rises, but the coral reef keeps growing upward so that its top just peeks above the waves.

The volcanic island has sunk from sight, but the coral reef remains in view. It forms a low, ring-shaped island called an atoll.

Sometimes you can see a volcanic island being born. In 1963 the island of Surtsey appeared off southwest Iceland.

Life near the surface

The sea is home to billions of plants and animals. Many live only near the sunlit surface. Sunlight gives plants the energy they need for making food. Plants in turn form food for animals, which only get food ready made, by eating plants or one another.

The most abundant organisms in oceans are the tiny plants and animals that form the plankton. The plants are known as phytoplankton, and the animals are called zooplankton. Plankton gets its name from a Greek word that means wandering: planktonic animals and plants just drift around with tides and currents. A bucket of sea water might hold a million microscopic diatoms – relatives of seaweeds encased in glassy boxes. Among planktonic animals are shrimp-like copepods, and radiolarians that look like little suns. Plankton also teems with baby jellyfish, worms, crabs, and fishes.

Larger, stronger swimmers such as fishes, squid, and whales eat planktonic animals or one another.

Herrings feed on copepods. Mackerel eat small herrings. Swordfish feed on mackerel. Each kind of creature is a link in a food chain of eaters and eaten. But herrings also get snapped up by seabirds, porpoises, and people. So the sea holds many food chains that interweave as food webs.

Plants and creatures of the sea also form food pyramids. In a food pyramid an immense number of plants forms the pyramid's broad base, supporting just one large creature at the top. It could take 100,000 tiny plants to feed 10,000 tiny animals. These might feed 1,000 young herrings, enough food for ten cod or one porpoise.

But the flow of food does not end here. Animals shed food wastes as droppings. Seabed creatures and bacteria break down the substances in droppings and in dead plant and animal remains. This releases minerals that fertilize the sea and help to nourish planktonic plants. So food goes around and around in a never-ending food cycle.

Microscopic plankton including radiolaria and diatoms.

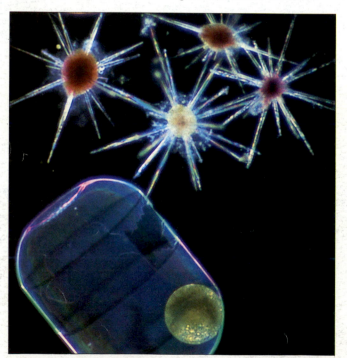

Killer whales near Vancouver, Canada.

Fish like these horse-eye jacks swim together in schools for protection.

Deep-sea life

The deeper you dive into an ocean, the darker it becomes, because water scatters and absorbs the sunlight shining from above. Even in the clearest sea almost all the light is lost 500 feet down. Only blue-black gloominess remains. Below 590 feet the ocean is as black as night.

At that depth the only plants that can grow are tiny single-celled algae. No one knows how even these exist without sunlight which is essential to all other plants. Yet the ocean depths are home to countless creatures. All somehow find enough to eat. Prawns, squid, and lantern fish swim up at night and catch tiny animals belonging to the plankton. Deep-sea fish gobble up each other, or they eat the squid and prawns when these dive down again. Worms, sea cucumbers, and shellfish live on or in the seabed mud, and suck up droppings or the remains of dead plants and creatures that have fallen onto the ocean floor from the surface far above.

Many deep-sea fish look extremely strange. Yet each is suited to life where food is scarce and darkness everlasting.

Lantern fish and stomiatoids glow with tiny lights. Certain other fish have silvery sides that act as mirrors. Lights and mirrors could help a fish to find a mate. They also attract prey and can confuse enemies.

Deep down big fish would not find enough to eat, so few fish grow much larger than your hand. But the tiny fish make the most of what there is. The angler fish lures victims with a kind of glowing fishing rod. *Astronesthes* sinks long, needle-sharp teeth into victims' bodies. Gulpers, swallowers, and deep-sea perches can stretch their jaws to swallow fishes even larger than themselves. Some of these tiny hunters of the deep seem to be all mouth or stomach. They need to be, to snatch a big meal when they get the chance. It might be weeks before they find another.

Left *Astronesthes* is a black fish with long fangs. Its body shines with many light-producing organs.

Right Each layer of the ocean tends to have its own set of creatures. Here are some examples in the different zones. Depth bands and sizes are not to scale, and cool-water and warm-water organisms are mixed.

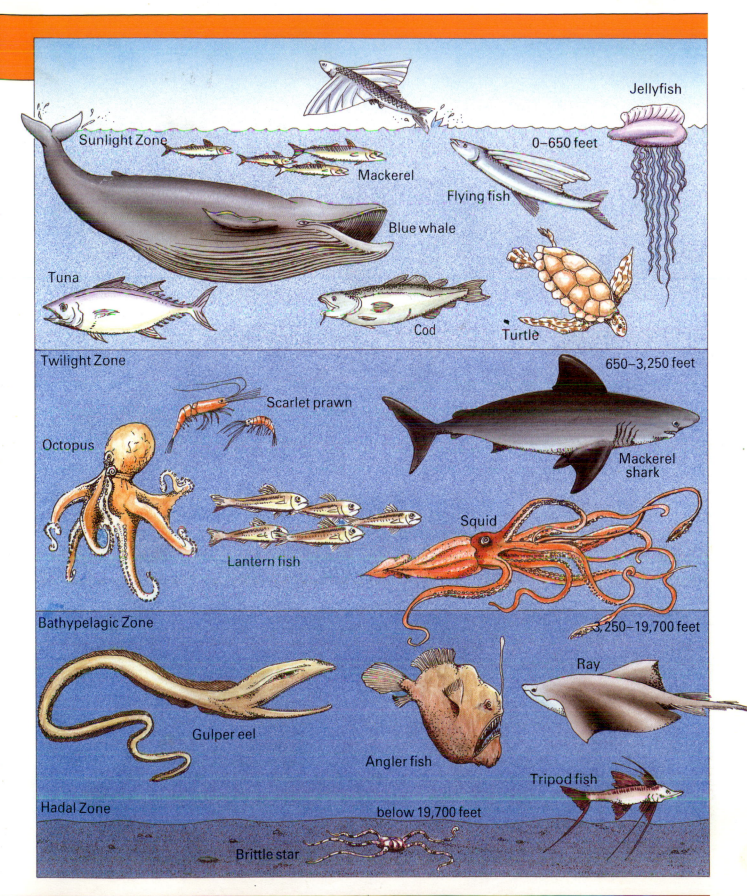

Jellyfish

Sunlight Zone

0–650 feet

Mackerel

Flying fish

Blue whale

Tuna

Cod

Turtle

Twilight Zone

650–3,250 feet

Scarlet prawn

Octopus

Mackerel shark

Squid

Lantern fish

Bathypelagic Zone

3,250–19,700 feet

Ray

Gulper eel

Angler fish

Tripod fish

Hadal Zone

below 19,700 feet

Brittle star

Life inshore

Seashores hold special opportunities and dangers for living things. Tides wash in plenty of food. But at low tide sea creatures run the risk of drying out. Storm waves batter shores, and temperatures can quickly soar and plunge. Seashore plants and creatures solve these problems, but most can cope with only one kind of shore.

Rocky shores are the chief homes of seaweeds. Seaweeds are algae, very simple plants that do not have roots, stems, and leaves like most land plants. The sea supports them so they do not need stiff cells. The part of a seaweed that looks like a root is called the holdfast. These holdfasts grip the rocks, to stop the seaweeds from being washed away.

Their floppy leaf-like fronds swish to and fro with the waves. When the tide drops, some seaweeds are left high and dry. But these rubbery plants stay moist and fresh until the sea comes in again.

Like seaweeds, sea anemones and shellfish grip rocks so hard that even storm waves cannot tear them loose. At low tide, sea anemones produce a sticky substance that keeps them moist, while barnacles and limpets stay moist inside their shells. But shore crabs and fish hide in rock pools.

When the tide comes in, feathery legs poke from the limpets' shells and grope for food particles. Then, too, the sea anemone opens its tentacles and catches shrimps or tiny fish.

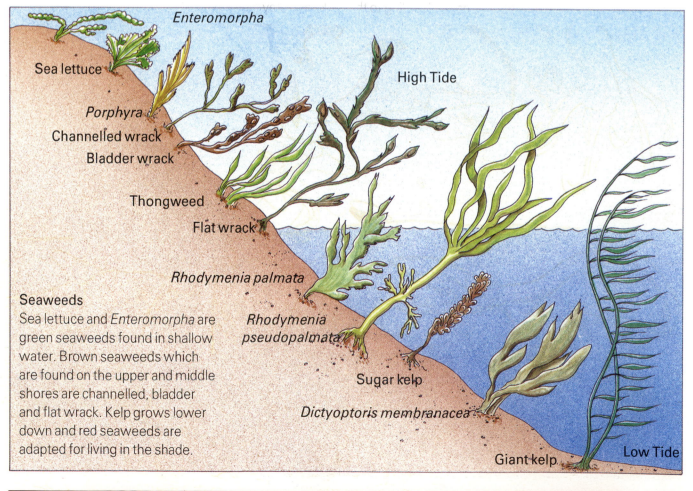

Enteromorpha

Sea lettuce

High Tide

Porphyra

Channelled wrack

Bladder wrack

Thongweed

Flat wrack

Rhodymenia palmata

Seaweeds
Sea lettuce and *Enteromorpha* are green seaweeds found in shallow water. Brown seaweeds which are found on the upper and middle shores are channelled, bladder and flat wrack. Kelp grows lower down and red seaweeds are adapted for living in the shade.

Rhodymenia pseudopalmata

Sugar kelp

Dictyoptoris membranacea

Giant kelp

Low Tide

Sea anemones produce a sticky substance to keep them moist when they are out of water.

Sandy shores have no firm rocks to cling to or hide under. Here, creatures burrow in the beach. At low tide, sea worms, razor shells, sea urchins, and shrimps lie safe and moist beneath the drying surface. When the sea returns, shrimps crawl out and swim around to feed. Big, hungry fish now make the inshore waters dangerous.

Creatures also burrow into muddy shores. Here live the little *Hydrobia* sea snails, big, ferocious ragworms, and strange opossum shrimps. Mud is rich in food, but it chokes breathing organs and lacks the oxygen that creatures need for breathing. Many burrowers in mud have special breathing tubes or filters.

When the tide goes out limpets and barnacles cling to the rocks and stay moist inside their shells.

Exploring under water

Once, people could only guess what lay below the waves. Now, underwater instruments and machines can tell us.

Some devices tell us about the water itself. Research ships lower bottles that fill with water at different levels in the sea. These Nansen bottles show the sea's saltiness at different depths. Thermometers fixed to the bottles measure the temperature at various levels. Ships tow bathythermographs to record how underwater temperature and pressure change across an ocean. Complicated devices called bathysondes measure underwater saltiness, temperature, pressure, and the speed of underwater sound. In order to learn how underwater currents flow, researchers use special buoys and floats that send back signals to the surface.

Yet other instruments explore the ocean bed. Echo-sounders on moving ships send down sound pulses and record the echoes bounced back from the bottom. These echoes show the ocean depth and help hydrographers to map the ocean floor. Grabs and dredges lowered on long lines can scoop up samples of deep-sea mud. Deep-sea drills can bring up long tube-shaped cores of sediment and rock from far below the surface of the ocean bed.

People wearing special diving suits can now explore shallow sea floors for themselves. Scuba divers swim around freely. But they breathe bottled air at the same high pressure as the water around them. After a deep dive they must spend days in a decompression chamber. Otherwise gas bubbles forming in their blood could kill or injure them.

People can dive far deeper in special underwater boats. In 1960 a kind of underwater balloon called a bathyscaphe took two men 6.7 miles to the bottom of the deepest ocean trench. Nowadays, small deep-sea vessels called submersibles are often used to explore the ocean floor. Submersibles can be manned or unmanned.

These French angel fish are swimming past a diver at Bonaire, in the West Indies.

This interior view of a submersible shows the equipment used for research.

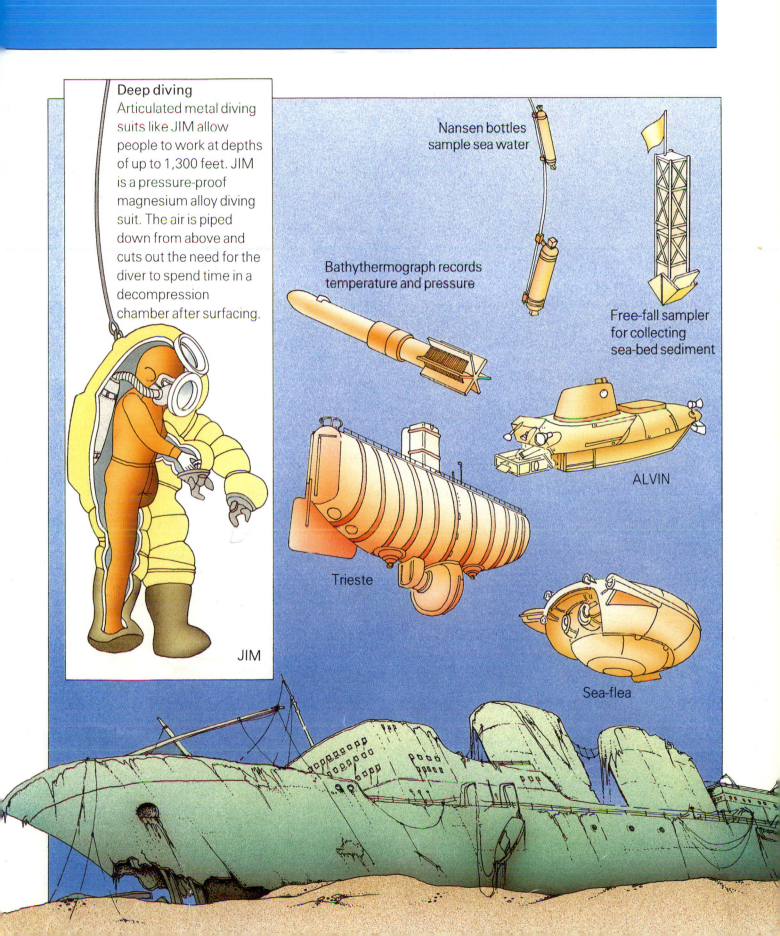

Deep diving
Articulated metal diving suits like JIM allow people to work at depths of up to 1,300 feet. JIM is a pressure-proof magnesium alloy diving suit. The air is piped down from above and cuts out the need for the diver to spend time in a decompression chamber after surfacing.

JIM

Nansen bottles sample sea water

Bathythermograph records temperature and pressure

Free-fall sampler for collecting sea-bed sediment

ALVIN

Trieste

Sea-flea

The Polynesians of the Pacific

The open ocean seems to be an unfriendly expanse of emptiness. When storms stir up huge waves it can be dangerous as well. Yet people have sailed the seas since Stone Age times in search of food and homes. The most successful of these ancient sailors were the Polynesians.

Today's Polynesians are the tall, light-skinned, dark-haired inhabitants of Polynesia, which means "many islands." Polynesia stretches from Hawaii to New Zealand and Easter Island. This vast triangle holds scores of smaller islands, scattered over thousands of miles of the Pacific Ocean.

Five thousand years ago the Polynesians' ancestors were fishermen and farmers who lived in southeast China, but they were daring sailors, too. By 2,000 years ago, they had canoed southeast beyond the Philippines to western Polynesia. By 1,000 years ago boatloads of families had peopled fertile, empty islands throughout the rest of Polynesia.

Family groups sailed and paddled over the Pacific in long canoes made of planks lashed edge-to-edge. Two canoes were often joined side-by-side to make one big double-hulled craft. Fishermen used smaller boats with an outrigger. This is a pole jutting from one side of a canoe to a floating log that balances the canoe. Boats of a similar design are still used today, as you can see in the photograph below.

Polynesian navigators had no compasses or other modern instruments to help them find their way. Instead, they learned to steer by the sun, stars, winds, and currents. They could sail to a tiny island which was far out of sight just by following different stars. The Polynesians even discovered distant unknown islands by observing the special color of the clouds above, and also by noticing where birds flew, or how the unseen islands made the waves behave. The Polynesians were undoubtedly the greatest navigators of the Stone Age world.

The Polynesians are famous sailors. This outrigger is sailing among the Pacific Islands.

These schoolgirls in French Polynesia are wearing beautiful garlands of exotic flowers.

The Long Trek

This map shows the likely journeys of Stone Age families who peopled the far-flung islands of Polynesia – the part of the Pacific Ocean bounded by Hawaii, Easter Island and New Zealand. By 1000 BC canoes from Fiji or nearby islands had reached uninhabited Samoa and Tonga. By AD 300 peoples from these islands had evidently sailed west to the Marquesas group. From this part of Polynesia, longer, and more dangerous and daring journeys took settlers to the farthest parts of Polynesia.

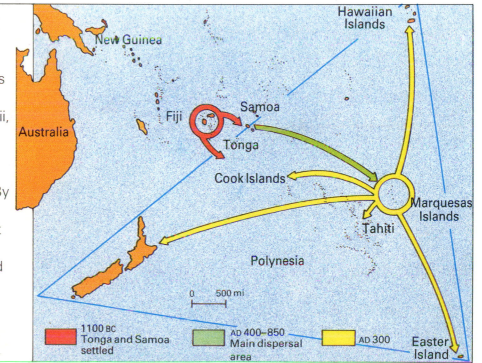

1100 BC
Tonga and Samoa settled

AD 400–850
Main dispersal area

AD 300

Ships and shipping

Earlier peoples had no way of crossing seas or oceans. But boats and ships slowly turned these watery barriers into highways.

Canoes or rafts probably took Old Stone Age families across a narrow sea gap from New Guinea to Australia as much as 40,000 years ago. By 4,500 years ago, small ships sailed along eastern Mediterranean coasts. But their square sails worked well only with the wind behind them, and ships easily lost their way unless they kept in sight of land.

By 500 years ago the Portuguese and Spanish had ships that sailed against the wind, and instruments that showed a ship's position out at sea. Brave sea captains began to cross the open oceans to find new trade routes to the spice-rich lands of southern Asia. In 1492 Christopher Columbus sailed all the way from Spain to North America. Between 1519 and 1522 Ferdinand Magellan's little Spanish ship *Victoria* became the first to circle the world.

Yet crossing oceans in small wooden sailing ships was slow and risky. Then, about a century ago, big metal steamships were built. These had engines to spin propellers that pushed water back to thrust these vessels forward. Such passenger ships took millions of Europeans to settle the almost empty lands of the Americas, Australia, and New Zealand.

Modern ships are powered by diesel motors, gas turbines, and other engines. Cruise liners and ferries still take passengers across seas, although most people crossing oceans travel by airplane. Today's biggest ships are cargo carriers. Immense oil tankers, ore carriers, and container ships carry enormous loads along busy sea lanes that criss-cross the water between the continents.

Many vessels pass through the great constructed waterways, the Panama and Suez canals. Between them, these short cuts save trips of thousands of miles around South America and southern Africa.

Inside an oil tanker

The engine, the crew's quarters, the control rooms and the navigating bridge are all at the stern (back) of the ship. This is so that they are as far away as possible from the dangerous cargo.

The oil-carrying space is divided into separate tanks so that different types of oil can be carried. This also means that if there is an accident it is less likely that all the cargo will be lost.

The enormous length of the tanker makes it very difficult to steer and control and the captain uses many electronic instruments to help him. A radar screen shows the course of the ship and others nearby, thus allowing the captain to steer his ship avoiding collision

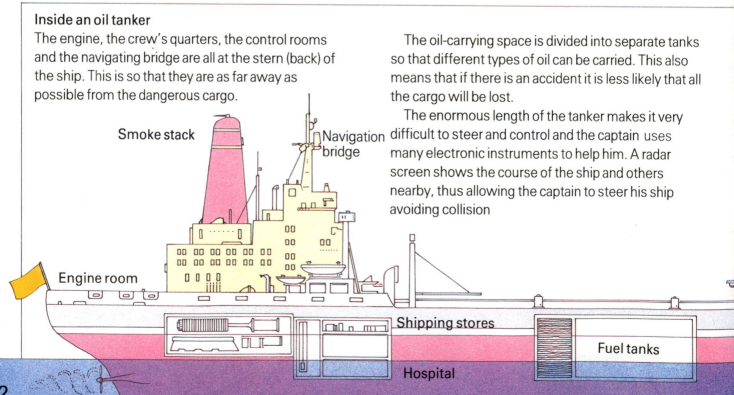

Smoke stack

Navigation bridge

Engine room

Shipping stores

Fuel tanks

Hospital

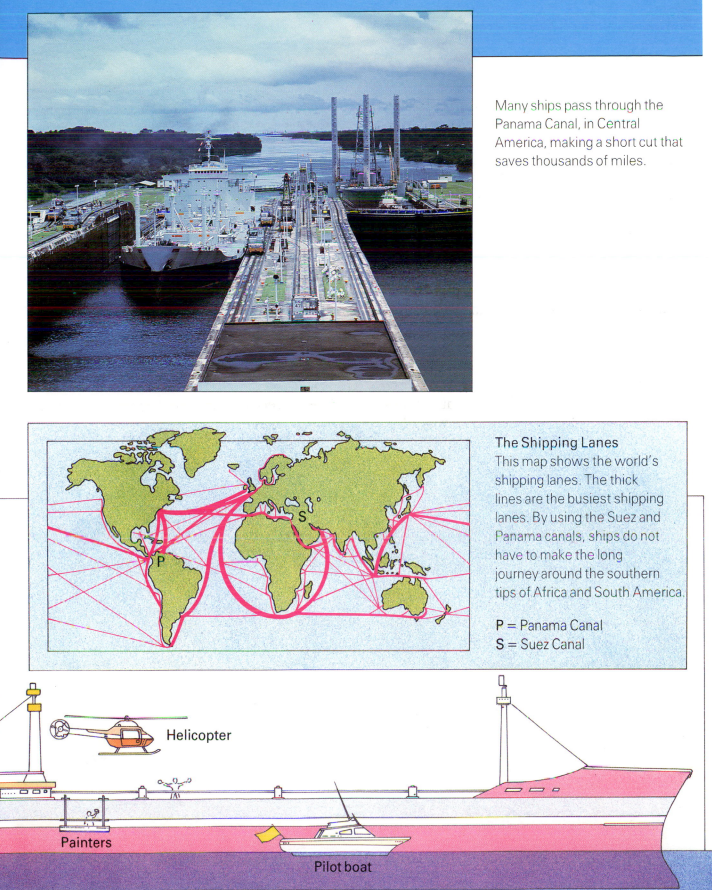

Many ships pass through the
Panama Canal, in Central
America, making a short cut that
saves thousands of miles.

The Shipping Lanes
This map shows the world's
shipping lanes. The thick
lines are the busiest shipping
lanes. By using the Suez and
Panama canals, ships do not
have to make the long
journey around the southern
tips of Africa and South America.

P = Panama Canal
S = Suez Canal

Helicopter

Painters

Pilot boat

Food from the sea

Fish and shellfish make nourishing and tasty foods. At first, fishermen just caught them from the shore in small amounts. Now, fishing ships sail the oceans and haul in more than 75 million tons of fish a year.

Rich fishing grounds lie where cold water wells up from the seafloor. The rising water brings minerals that nourish the plankton that fish depend on for food. But fishermen catch different fish at different levels in the sea. Herring, mackerel, sardines, and tuna swim near the surface. Cod, haddock, Alaskan pollack, plaice, and turbot swim on the shallow floors of continental shelves.

Once, fishermen cast nets and lines by guesswork. Now experts can map fishes' migration routes and spawning grounds. And fishing craft with sonar instruments can detect shoals of fishes miles away.

A long-range fishing fleet may include several small catcher craft and a big factory ship. The catcher craft pass fish to the factory ship, where the fish are frozen to keep them fresh.

Sea fish are still caught by hunting, but now there are seafood farmers, too. Off certain coasts people grow mussels and oysters on sticks stuck in the seabed, or on lines that hang from rafts. The Japanese grow edible seaweed on fixed underwater nets in Japan's shallow Inland Sea. Farming seafood provides a more reliable food supply than fishing. If overhunting reduces the world's fish catch, seafood farming will become more and more important.

Catching "new" sea foods is another way of increasing food supplies. Antarctic fishing fleets already net huge quantities of shrimp-like krill. Soon, perhaps, unusual fish like black scabbard, grenadier, and kapelin could reach our plates.

Edible seaweed is cultivated on nets in Japan's shallow Inland Sea. This is Gokasho Bay, Shimo Peninsula.

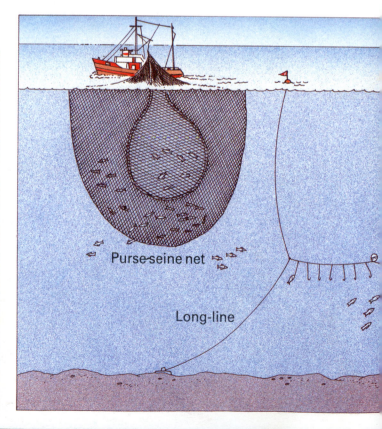

Purse-seine net

Long-line

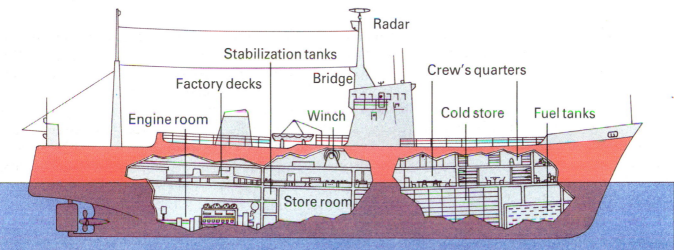

Radar

Stabilization tanks

Factory decks

Bridge

Crew's quarters

Engine room

Winch

Cold store

Fuel tanks

Store room

Sea fishing

Different methods of fishing catch different groups of fish (**below**). Trawling nets along the seabed trap bottom-living fish. Purse-seine nets can trap a shoal of fish at the surface. Long drift nets, hanging like a curtain, catch surface swimmers. Long-lining uses hooks hung from long lines.

The freezer trawler

The diagram, **above**, shows the layout of a typical freezer trawler capable of quick-freezing tons of fish at sea

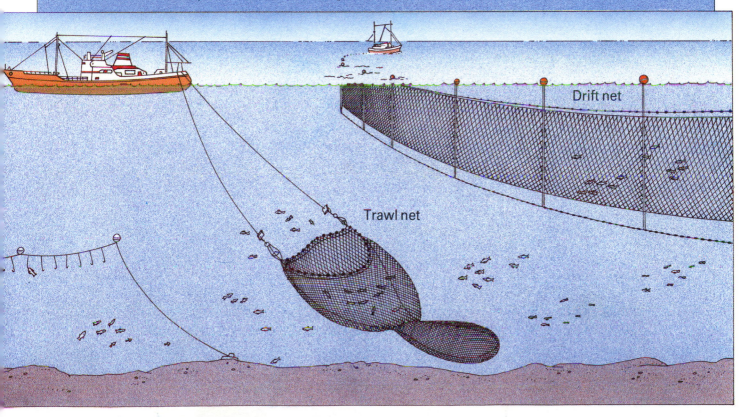

Drift net

Trawl net

Mining the sea

Seawater and the seafloor hold many useful substances, but only some can be extracted and separated in useful quantities.

Water is the most plentiful ingredient in the sea, but it is too salty to drink. Places with special equipment called desalination plants can separate water from salt. They heat the brine and cool the steam that boils away, until it turns into pure water. In some desert countries, desalination plants are used to make water for drinking and irrigation.

The second most plentiful ingredient in the sea is salt. People collect sea salt by pumping brine into shallow pools called pans where sun and wind evaporate the water. When all the water has evaporated, a crust of salt remains.

Most of the world's magnesium and bromine also come from seawater. Magnesium goes to make strong, light metal alloys. Bromine is used for making medicines, dyes, and photographs.

Seawater even contains gold and silver, but in amounts too small to be worth extracting.

Below the sea itself, parts of the continental shelves are rich in gravels, sands, and tin. Dredging vessels armed with powerful pumps suck up great loads of these materials and dump them into waiting barges.

Huge quantities of oil and gas lie trapped in layered rocks below shallow waters such as the North Sea and the Gulf of Mexico. Engineers use equipment to drill down to the oil and gas, from platforms perched above the sea on very long, strong steel or concrete legs. The oil or gas then flows through pipes to waiting tankers, or ashore.

The deep floor of the open ocean also has its riches. Here lie millions of metallic lumps called manganese nodules. Deep-sea dredging vessels could suck or scoop them to the surface. Such deep-sea mining is expensive. But it might become worthwhile if mines on land ran out of manganese (a substance used to harden steel). The nodules also hold other useful elements, particularly aluminum, cobalt, copper, lead, and nickel.

People have been separating salt from seawater for thousands of years. These men are harvesting salt at Trofari in Sicily, Italy.

Far right A production platform in the West Sole gas field in the North Sea.

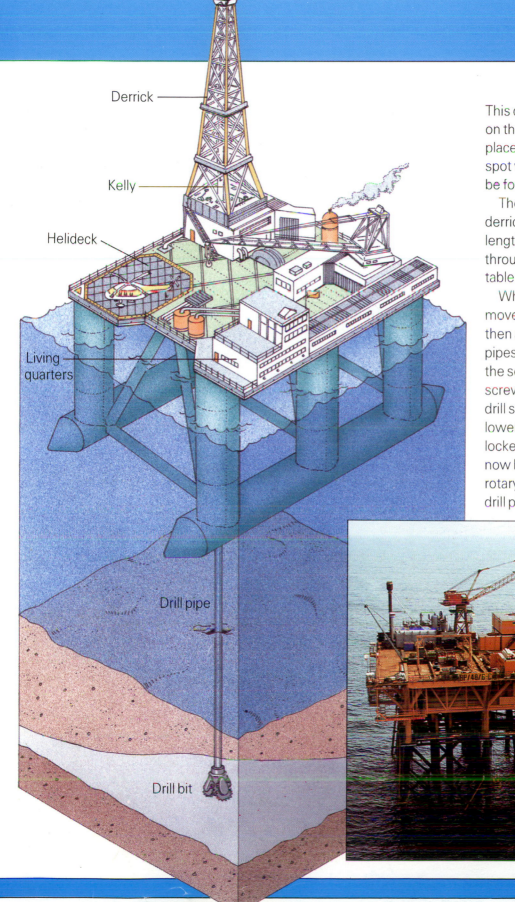

Derrick

Kelly

Helideck

Living quarters

Drill pipe

Drill bit

This drilling platform or oil rig floats on the sea and can be moved from place to place. It is anchored over a spot where scientists think oil may be found in the seabed.

The tall metal tower is called the derrick. Inside this is the kelly, a length of square pipe which fits through a square hole in the rotary table at the base of the derrick.

When work begins, the kelly is moved out of the way. A drill bit is then attached to a series of drill pipes until the drill almost reaches the seabed. The top drill pipe is then screwed to the kelly. Next the whole drill string (kelly, drill pipes, and bit) is lowered until the foot of the kelly is locked in the rotary table. Drilling can now begin and an engine turns the rotary table which turns the kelly, drill pipes, and bit.

Seas in danger

Two kinds of danger threaten seas and oceans. One comes from adding harmful wastes. The other danger comes from taking out too many fish and shellfish from the oceans.

Each year oil tankers and offshore oil rigs spill millions of tons of oil into the sea. The oil is sometimes washed up onto our shores, ruining the beaches. A big oil spill can also kill millions of sea creatures, and drown or suffocate thousands of sea birds.

Every day, factories, farms, and towns allow left-over poisonous substances to flow into the sea. In the 1950s and 1960s, factories poured mercury waste into Japan's Minamata Bay. The local people ate the shellfish that had been contaminated by the mercury. As mercury is very poisonous, the people who ate the shellfish suffered brain damage, blindness, loss of muscle power, or death.

Fertilizers and pesticides used on farms are washed off the land and into the sea by rivers. Pesticides that are sprayed on the land contaminate the air, and enter the sea by offshore winds and rain. Today, fishes' bodies are still accumulating DDT and other dangerous pesticides which were washed off the land into the sea by rivers years ago – before we knew that people and creatures who ate fish contaminated with DDT could accumulate dangerous concentrations of these poisons in their own bodies.

Some towns and cities pour untreated sewage into the sea. Untreated sewage can carry germs causing dangerous diseases such as typhoid. The sewage also acts as a fertilizer that helps tiny floating plants multiply. When these die they rot. But rotting uses up the oxygen in water. Too little oxygen remains for healthy water plants and

Pollution in the Mediterranean Sea

The Mediterranean is an almost enclosed sea into which many nations pour all kinds of wastes. Much of the pollution comes from raw sewage and factory wastes poured into the sea through pipes or rivers from big industrial centers. Because the sea is almost enclosed these wastes tend to accumulate and pollute the waters, suffocating or poisoning sea creatures. They may also cause illnesses in people who bathe on certain beaches or eat certain kinds of sea creatures – particularly shellfish such as oysters. Some parts of the Mediterranean are more seriously affected than others. Our map shows areas most at risk from pollution by sewage and oil spills.

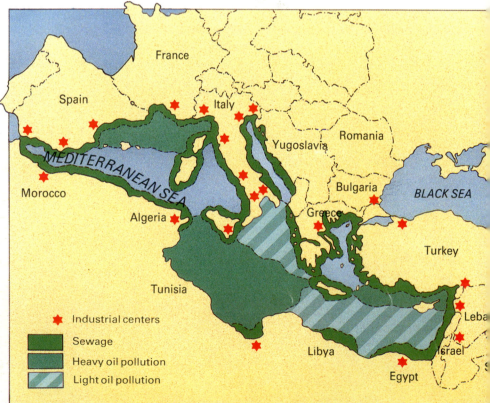

★ Industrial centers

▮ Sewage

▮ Heavy oil pollution

▨ Light oil pollution

Man can threaten the existence of some species by overfishing. These pilot whales are being slaughtered in the Faroe Islands, in the North Atlantic.

animals to breathe and as a result they also die.

Such substances that spoil the sea are called pollutants. Pollution has been particularly bad in parts of those shallow, almost enclosed seas — the Baltic and Mediterranean. Scientists have warned that both could turn into lifeless, smelly wastes.

Overfishing is a danger both to seas and open oceans. In the North Sea, and parts of the North Atlantic, fishermen have caught fish like cod or herring in such large quantities that the fish have not been able to breed fast enough to replace the number taken out. Off the coast of Peru, the once huge catches of anchovies dwindled to a fraction of their size, partly because too many ships were hunting them. In the cold waters of the world's far south, Japanese and Russian whaling ships have caught so many whales that certain kinds might die out altogether.

We still have time to save the seas, but, unhappily, poor countries cannot afford the cost of keeping offshore waters clean. The open ocean may be healthy, but some shallow seas are still at risk.

These sea birds have been drowned in oil from a tanker spill.

Saving the sea

Scientists have proved that dumping wastes and overfishing harm the seas and oceans. Friends of the Earth, Greenpeace, and other conservation groups have helped to spread the news. Now, conservationists, manufacturers, and governments have set to work to try to stop the damage.

There are many ways in which this can be done. For instance, special precautions help to prevent oil spills when oil tankers load or clean their tanks. Keeping in the right shipping lane cuts down the risk of ships colliding and spilling poisonous cargoes. Purifying sewage and factory wastes on land can make them safe to be released into the sea. Sealing nuclear waste in special glass containers and burying these on land should keep their poisons from leaking out and harming fish. Using safer pesticides than DDT means that rivers already carry less poison from farms into the sea.

But we shall only clean the seas if countries work together. In 1975 the United Nations persuaded sixteen Mediterranean countries to agree to stop pouring poisonous wastes into their sea. By the middle 1980s other nations had agreed to clean up most of nine other danger areas.

Meanwhile, countries were passing laws to stop fishing vessels from catching threatened fish stocks in their offshore waters. Such laws may well have saved the North Atlantic cod and herring, and the Peruvian anchovy. Whaling nations have themselves banned hunting endangered whales, perhaps in time to save these threatened species.

To keep lovely coral reefs safe from interference, several countries, which include Australia and the United States, have declared some offshore areas reserves or national parks, whose plants and animals must be protected.

National parks protect areas from pollution by people. This is Port Campbell National Park, Victoria, Australia.

Left Greenpeace protesters in an inflatable dinghy try to hamper the progress of a whaling ship.

Below Oil spills from wrecked tankers cause terrible pollution. Here oil from the Torrey Canyon disaster is being sprayed with detergent. But detergent itself is also a pollutant.

Harnessing seas and oceans

Human beings are tiny compared with seas or oceans, and weak compared with tides and waves. Yet we have the know-how and machines to wall-off seas and put the waves and tides to work.

Each day, the world's waves strike its shores with immense force. Tides, too, release vast quantities of energy. Scientists have plans to turn this energy into electric current for our homes.

Already, French engineers have built a tidal barrage (a kind of wall) across the mouth of the Rance River. As the tide surges to and fro through holes in the wall, it spins propellers called turbine blades. These spinning turbines generate electricity. China and the Soviet Union have tidal power stations too, and there are plans for more.

Harnessing the North Atlantic's wild waves is harder than harnessing tides. But Norwegian scientists have built an underwater "lens" to concentrate waves and raise water into a high-level reservoir. Water falling from this reservoir spins turbine blades to generate electric current. British scientists have other plans. But most would need many miles of floating rafts or air bags.

Meanwhile engineers have plans to tamper with the seas themselves. The Dutch have reclaimed two-fifths of their country from the sea by building dykes around lakes of shallow sea water and pumping the water into canals. The canals take the water to the sea beyond the dykes. These drained areas, or polders, become rich farmland. Now

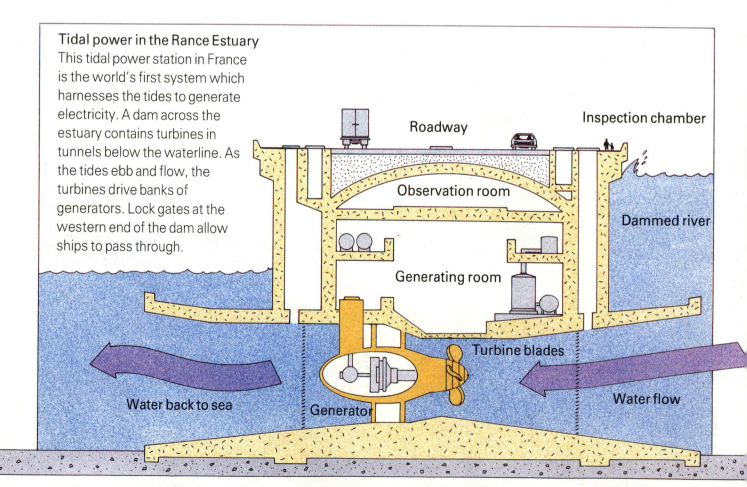

Tidal power in the Rance Estuary
This tidal power station in France is the world's first system which harnesses the tides to generate electricity. A dam across the estuary contains turbines in tunnels below the waterline. As the tides ebb and flow, the turbines drive banks of generators. Lock gates at the western end of the dam allow ships to pass through.

Roadway

Inspection chamber

Observation room

Dammed river

Generating room

Turbine blades

Water back to sea

Generator

Water flow

Vast areas of the Netherlands have been reclaimed from the sea and now provide rich farmland.

British, Dutch, and Japanese engineers want to build ports or airports on artificial islands in the sea.

Some engineers have thought up even grander schemes. In 1928 one German engineer suggested building a wall across the western Mediterranean. Atlantic Ocean water would stop flowing into the Mediterranean, so that sea would shrink, and leave new land around its rim.

Such costly schemes may never take place. But by the year 2000, Soviet engineers might have made some rivers flow south, instead of north, into the Arctic Ocean.

Vast changes could affect the seas within your lifetime. The seas and oceans could become a major source of food and energy.

In France engineers have built a tidal barrage across the Rance River near St. Malo.

Carrying sharks to market, India.

Glossary

Abyss   A deep ocean floor and its waters.
Atoll   A low island made of a ring-shaped coral reef.
Bathyscaphe   A pressure-resistant undersea craft for use in the deep ocean. A type of submersible.
Bathysonde   An instrument for measuring underwater temperature, pressure, saltiness, and the speed of sound.
Bathythermograph   An instrument for measuring underwater temperature and pressure.
Brine   Very salty water.
Buoy   A floating object used for giving information. Many buoys are aids to navigation.
Contaminate   To make impure.
Continental drift   The slow drift of continents across the earth, with the crustal plates they rest upon.
Continental rise   The gentle slope at the foot of a continental slope.
Continental shelf   The underwater shelf that juts out into the sea around a continent.
Continental slope   The slope leading from the continental shelf down to the continental rise.
Coriolis effect   The way that currents (and winds) are steered by the earth's spin.
Crust   The hard, rocky surface of the earth.
Decompression chamber   A room where divers gradually become accustomed to atmospheric pressures, after having been under great pressure in the ocean depths. Being in the chamber prevents the divers from becoming ill.
Delta   The triangular, flat area at the mouth of some rivers, where the mainstream divides into several smaller channels.
Desalination   The removal of salt from water.
Drought   A prolonged period with hardly any rain.
Dyke   An embankment constructed to prevent flooding or keep out the sea.
Echo-sounder   A device for detecting the depth of the seabed or other underwater objects.
Estuary   A broad, low, river mouth.
Euphotic zone   The uppermost part of a sea or lake, down to about 325 feet depth.

Extract   To take out.
Gyre   A "loop" of ocean currents flowing around an ocean.
Hydrographer   Someone who studies, surveys, and makes maps of the oceans, seas, and rivers.
Iceberg   A mass of ice that has fallen into the sea.
Lagoon   An area of shallow water separated from the sea by a narrow strip of land.
Manganese nodule   A lump of manganese and other substances, lying on the ocean floor. The nodules form when chemicals dissolved in water stick to objects such as fishes' teeth.
Mantle   The hot, dense layer of rock below the earth's crust.
Ooze   Liquid mud.
Organism   Any living animal or plant.
Overfishing   Catching fish faster than they can breed, so causing their numbers to dwindle.
Pesticide   A chemical used for killing plant or animal pests.
Plankton   Drifting, mostly tiny, plants and creatures that live at the ocean surface.
Plates   Crustal plates are the great slabs that form the earth's crust. Some carry continents.
Pollution   The spoiling of water, air, or land by harmful substances.
Reef   A rock ridge just under or above the sea.
Scuba   Self-contained underwater breathing apparatus.
Seaweed   One of the group of simple plants called algae.
Sediments   Substances like mud and sand that have settled on the bottom of a sea, lake, or river.
Spreading ridge   An underwater mountain chain formed of volcanic rock that rises in the crack between two separating crustal plates.
Submersible   A small manned or unmanned diving vessel. Unlike submarines, submersibles keep much of their equipment outside the pressurized hull that holds the crew.
Swell   A long, rounded wave produced by far-off winds or storms.

Tides   Huge waves that travel around the earth twice a day as a result of the forces of the sun and the moon acting on the rotating earth.

Trench   An ocean trench is a deep gash in the ocean floor.

Tsunami   A huge ocean wave set off by an underwater earthquake or volcanic eruption.

United Nations   An international organization to promote peace and international cooperation and security.

Water cycle   The flow of water vapor and water that produces clouds, rain, and rivers, and keeps the ocean full.

Wave   A disturbance passing through the surface of the sea or land.

Further reading

Bramwell, Martin, *Oceans* (Franklin Watts, 1984).

Carson, Rachel, *The Sea Around Us* (Oxford University Press, 1961).

Cook, Jan L., *The Mysterious Undersea World* (National Geographic, 1980).

Davies, Eryl, *Ocean Frontiers* (Viking Press, 1980).

Hargreaves, Pat, *Seas and Oceans* series – 8 titles (Silver Burdett Press, 1980/81).

Polking, Kirk, *Oceans of the World: Our Essential Resource* (Putnam, 1983).

Roux, Charles, *Animals of the Seashore* (Silver Burdett, 1983).

Roux, Charles and Plantain, Paul-Henry, *Ocean Dwellers* (Silver Burdett Press, 1983).

Rutland, Jonathan, *The Sea* (Silver Burdett, 1983).

Sandok, Cass R., *The World's Oceans* (Franklin Watts, 1986).

Picture acknowledgments

The publishers would like to thank the following for allowing their photographs to be reproduced in this book: Bruce Coleman 4 (NASA), 15 (left/Jennifer Fry), 17 (Robert Burton), 22 (right/David Wrigglesworth) 28 (left) and *front cover* (inset) (M. Timothy O'Keefe), 30, 36 (Nicholas Devore), 34 (Orion Press), 39 (R.J. Tulloch); Geoscience Features Library 7, 19, 21; Greenpeace 41; The Hutchison Library 13 (below), 40; Oxford Scientific Films 9 (G.H. Thompson), 13 (above/Laurence Gould), 15 (right/Godfrey Merlen), 16 (Peter O'Toole), 22 (left/Peter Parks), 27 (both/G.I. Bernard); Planet Earth/Seaphot 11 (both/John Lythgoe), 25 (Peter David), 28 (right/Ken Vaughan), 39 (Rob Beighton), 41 (Geoff Harwood); TOPHAM 43; Wayland Picture Library 37; ZEFA *back cover, front cover* (main picture), 7, 31, 38. All illustrations are by Stefan Chabluk.

Index

Abyss 18
Africa 5, 12, 32
Alaska 10
Amazon River 6
Angler fish 24
Antarctica 5, 20
Arctic Ocean 5, 6, 43
Asia 14, 20, 32
Astronesthes 24
Atlantic Ocean 4, 5, 14, 18, 20, 39, 43
Atoll 20
Australia 5, 20, 32, 40

Baltic Sea 10, 38
Bathyscaphe 28
Bathysondes 28
Bathythermograph 28
Bay of Fundy 10
Benguela Current 12
Bivalves 27
Black Sea 14
Boats 32
Borneo 20
Brine 36
Bromine 36

Canada 10, 11
Canaries Current 12
Caribbean Sea 5, 12, 20
Caspian Sea 4, 14
Catspaws 8
China 42
Cliffs 16
Coasts 16
Columbus, Christopher 32
Conservation 40
Continental crust 14
Continental drift 20
Continental rise 18
Continental shelf 18, 28, 36

Coral reef 20
Coriolis effect 12
Coriolis, Gaspard de 12
Crustal plate 14
Currents 12, 16, 28

DDT 39, 40
Dead Sea 4, 6
Decompression chamber 28
Deep-sea life 24
Deep-sea perch 24
Desalination 36
Diatoms 22
Dredges 28
Drift-netting 34

Echo-sounders 28
Euphotic zone 22
Europe 5, 14, 18, 20

Ferries 32
Fertilizers 38
Fishermen 34, 39
Fishing 34
Food chain 22
Food pyramid 22
Food web 22
French angel fish 28
Friends of the Earth 40

Gold 36
Great Barrier Reef 20
Great Britain 20
Greenland 20
Greenpeace 40
Gulf of Mexico 10, 12, 36
Gulf Stream 12
Gulper fish 24
Gyres 12

Hawaiian Islands 20

Herrings 22, 34
Humboldt Current 12
Hydrobia 27
Hydrographer 28
Hydrological cycle 6

Icebergs 7
Iceland 18
Indian Ocean 4, 5, 20
Ireland 20

Japan 20, 34, 38
Java 20
Jellyfish 22

Lantern fish 24
Lateika 20
Limpets 26, 27
Long-lining 34

Mackerel 22, 34
Magellan, Ferdinand 32
Magnesium 36
Manganese nodules 35
Mantle 14
Mediterranean Sea 5, 10, 32, 38, 43
Mid-Atlantic Ridge 14, 18
Migration route 34
Minamata Bay 38
Mindanao Trench 5
Minerals 6, 34
Molten rock 14
Mount Everest 5, 19
Mudflats 17
Mussels 34

Nansen bottle 28
Neap-tide 10
Nekton 22
Netherlands 43
New Guinea 32

New Zealand 20, 32
North Atlantic Drift 12
North Atlantic gyre 12
North Equatorial Current 12
North Sea 36, 38
Nuclear waste 40

Ocean floor 14, 18
Oil 36
Oil tankers 32, 36, 38, 40
Ooze 19
Outrigger 30, 31
Oxygen 22, 38
Oysters 34

Pacific Ocean 4, 5, 8, 14, 18, 20, 30
Panama Canal 32, 33
Pangaea 14, 20
Peninsulas 17
Peru 12
Pesticides 38
Plankton 23, 34
Plates 14
Polders 43
Pollution 38, 39
Polynesians 30, 31
Porpoises 22
Prawns 24
Purse-seining 34

Radiolarians 22
Ragworms 27
Rance barrage 42
Razor shells 27
Red Sea 6
Russia 42

Salt 6
Sardines 14
Scuba diver 28

Sea anemones 26, 27
Sea cucumbers 24
Seafood farmers 34
Seaweeds 22, 26
Sediments 18
Sewage 38, 40
Shellfish 24, 34, 38
Shipping lanes 33
Ships 32, 33
Silver 36
Sodium chloride 6
South America 32
Spain 32
Spawning ground 34
Spring-tide 10
Squid 22, 24
Steamships 32
Stomiatoids 24
Submersibles 28, 29
Suez Canal 32
Sumatra 20
Swallower fish 24

Tides 10, 18, 42
Trawling 34
Tropics 12
Tsunami 8
Tuna 34
Typhoid 38

United Nations 40
United States 12, 14, 32, 40

Water cycle 6
Water vapor 6
Waves 8, 16, 18, 26, 42
West Indies 18
Whales 22, 39, 40
Whaling ships 39